HOW&WHY?

ANIMALS HATCH FROM EGGS

Elaine Pascoe is the author of more than 20 acclaimed children's books on a wide range of subjects.
Dwight Kuhn's scientific expertise and artful eye work together with the camera to capture the awesome wonder of the natural world.

Please visit our web site at: www.garethstevens.com
For a free color catalog describing Gareth Stevens Publishing's list of high-quality books
and multimedia programs, call 1-800-542-2595 or fax your request to (414) 332-3567.

Library of Congress Cataloging-in-Publication Data

Pascoe, Elaine.
    Animals hatch from eggs / by Elaine Pascoe; photographs by Dwight Kuhn. — North American ed.
      p. cm. — (How & why: a springboards into science series)
    Includes bibliographical references and index.
    Summary: Explains how animals protect their eggs and why some animals lay their eggs in
special places.
    ISBN 0-8368-3004-0 (lib. bdg.)
    1. Embryology—Juvenile literature. 2. Eggs—Juvenile literature. [1. Embryology. 2. Eggs.]
    I. Kuhn, Dwight, ill. II. Title.
QL956.5.P37   2002
571.8'61—dc21   2001049478

This North American edition first published in 2002 by
Gareth Stevens Publishing
A World Almanac Education Group Company
330 West Olive Street, Suite 100
Milwaukee, WI 53212 USA

First published in the United States in 2000 by Creative Teaching Press, Inc., P.O. Box 2723, Huntington Beach, CA 92647-0723.
Text © 2000 by Elaine Pascoe; photographs © 2000 by Dwight Kuhn. Additional end matter © 2002 by Gareth Stevens, Inc.

Gareth Stevens editor: Mary Dykstra
Gareth Stevens designer: Tammy Gruenewald

Printed in the United States of America

1 2 3 4 5 6 7 8 9 06 05 04 03 02

HOW & WHY?

ANIMALS HATCH FROM EGGS

by Elaine Pascoe

photographs by Dwight Kuhn

Gareth Stevens Publishing

A WORLD ALMANAC EDUCATION GROUP COMPANY

A hen lays her eggs in a nest of straw. The hen's babies, or chicks, grow inside the eggs. The hen sits on the nest, covering the eggs with her feathers. She must keep the eggs warm until they are ready to hatch.

Like chickens, all birds hatch from eggs. Frogs, salamanders, and many fish, snakes, and insects hatch from eggs, too. An egg is a perfect place for a growing baby. Its shell protects the baby, and its yolk provides all the food the baby needs.

Three weeks after a hen lays an egg, the chick inside the egg is ready to come out. The chick uses its beak to chip a hole in the egg's hard shell. Then it keeps chipping, all the way around the shell.

Finally, the chick pushes the broken shell apart and greets the world. Its downy feathers are wet, but they will soon be dry and fluffy.

A green snake hides her eggs in a rotting log and slithers away. She does not stay to take care of the eggs. When a baby snake is ready to hatch, it pushes through the egg's thick, leathery shell.

The baby snake can live on its own right away. It already knows how to hunt for insects and other small prey.

A spotted salamander lays her eggs in water and coats the eggs with jelly. The jelly protects the eggs and keeps them attached to an underwater branch.

When the young salamanders hatch, they wriggle out of the jelly. They will spend the first part of their lives in water. As they grow older, they will move to land.

A painted turtle lays her eggs in a shallow hole she makes in sandy soil. The turtle covers the eggs with sand to hide them from birds and other animals that might eat them. Then the turtle goes back to her pond.

When the baby turtles hatch, they climb out of their sandy nest and head for the water.

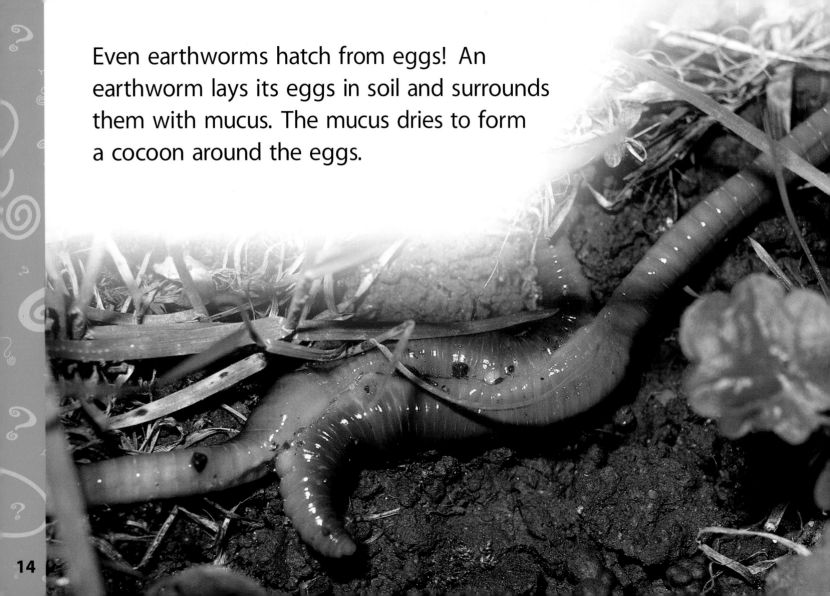

Even earthworms hatch from eggs! An earthworm lays its eggs in soil and surrounds them with mucus. The mucus dries to form a cocoon around the eggs.

The cocoon lies in the ground for about three weeks.
Then tiny, new earthworms hatch and wriggle away.

A ladybug lays its eggs on the underside of a plant leaf. The ladybug chooses the plant carefully to make sure it is a plant that will have aphids on it. Aphids are tiny insects that feed on plant juices. They are also the ladybug's favorite prey.

As soon as they hatch, young ladybugs, called larvae, start hunting aphids. After the larvae develop into adult ladybugs, they will lay eggs of their own.

Can you answer these "HOW & WHY" questions?

1. Why does a hen sit on her eggs?

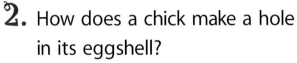

2. How does a chick make a hole in its eggshell?

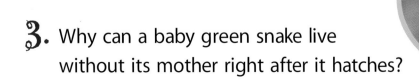

3. Why can a baby green snake live without its mother right after it hatches?

4. How does a spotted salamander protect her eggs?

5. Why does a painted turtle cover her eggs with sand?

6. Why do ladybugs lay their eggs on plants that have aphids?

(See page 20 for answers.)

ANSWERS

1. A hen sits on her eggs to keep them warm until the babies inside them are fully developed and ready to hatch.

2. A chick has a point on its beak, called an egg tooth, that is sharp enough to chip through the egg's hard shell.

3. When a baby green snake hatches, it already knows how to find its own food.

4. A spotted salamander coats her eggs with a special protective jelly.

5. A painted turtle covers her eggs with sand to hide them from birds and other animals that might eat them.

6. A ladybug's larvae need to eat as soon as they hatch, and aphids are their favorite food.

Eggs Over Easy

Make a concentration memory game of animals that hatch from eggs. Ask an adult to help you cut egg shapes out of twenty index cards. On ten of the cards, write the names of ten animals that hatch from eggs. Put one animal name on each card. On each remaining card, draw a picture of one of the animals so that each animal named also has a picture card. Turn over all of the cards so you cannot see the names and pictures. With another player, take turns turning over two cards, trying to find matching names and pictures. If you find a match, keep the set of cards. If you do not find a match, turn both cards down again and let the other player take a turn. When all the cards are matched, the player with the most sets wins.

An Eggs-cellent Egg

Animal eggs come in many shapes, sizes, and colors. Find pictures of different kinds of eggs and learn why some eggs are certain colors or particular shapes. Then, pretending that your bedroom is a bird's habitat, use crayons or markers to design an egg suitable for that habitat.

A Practical Yolk

Eggs sold in grocery stores do not have baby chicks growing inside them. Ask an adult to help you break open an egg so you can study its parts. Find the yellow yolk and the clear, slimy albumen, or egg white. Also look for the chalaza, which is the twisted white string that holds the egg yolk in place. Learn the purpose for each part of the egg.

GLOSSARY

aphids: tiny, licelike insects that damage plants by sucking out their juices.

chip (v): to break off in small pieces.

coats: covers a surface with a layer of a liquid substance.

cocoon: a protective covering that wraps completely around something like the silky case a caterpillar makes for shelter while it is changing into a moth.

downy: soft and fluffy like the feathers of a baby chick.

fluffy: light and soft like a cotton ball or the feathers of a baby bird.

hatch (v): to come, or break, out of an egg.

jelly: a smooth, gooey, liquid substance that has no defined shape.

larvae: the wingless, wormlike form of an insect when it first hatches from an egg.

leathery: looking or feeling like leather.

mucus: a thick, slimy fluid that coats and protects the inside of some body parts.

pond: a body of water smaller than a lake.

prey (n): an animal that is hunted by another animal for food.

rotting: decaying and falling apart.

shallow: not deep.

shell: a hard outer covering that protects something inside.

slithers: slides smoothly over the ground or some other surface.

surrounds: closes in on all sides.

wriggle: move quickly in short bursts from side to side; wiggle; squirm.

yolk: the part of an egg that contains food for a developing baby animal.

More Books to Read

Animals and Their Eggs. Animals Up Close (series). Renne (Gareth Stevens)
An Earthworm's Life. John Himmelman (Children's Press)
Egg to Chick. Millicent E. Selsam (Econo-Clad Books)
Ladybug. Life Cycles (series). David M. Schwartz (Gareth Stevens)
A Nest Full of Eggs. Priscilla Belz Jenkins (HarperCollins)
The Wonder of Butterflies. Amy Bauman and E. Jaediker Norsgaard (Gareth Stevens)

Videos

Amazing Animals: Animal Eggs. (DK Vision)
Babies of the Pond. (Library Video)
Bug City: Incredible Insects! (Schlessinger Media)

Web Sites

www.lizardboy.com/eggs/eggs.html
www.parks.tas.gov.au/wildlife/mammals/platypus.html
www.poultryclub.org/VHIncubation.htm

Some web sites stay current longer than others. For additional web sites, use a good search engine to locate the following topics: *birds, eggs, hatching, incubation,* and *insects.*

INDEX

aphids 16, 17

babies 4, 8, 9, 13
birds 4, 12

chickens 4, 6, 7
cocoons 14, 15

earthworms 14, 15

feathers 4, 7
fish 4
frogs 4

hatching 4, 8, 11, 13, 14, 15, 17

insects 4, 9, 16

jelly 10, 11

ladybugs 16, 17
larvae 17

mucus 14

plants 16
prey 9, 16

salamanders 4, 10, 11
sand 12, 13
shells 4, 6, 7, 8
snakes 4, 8, 9
soil 12, 14

turtles 12, 13

water 10, 11, 13

yolks 4